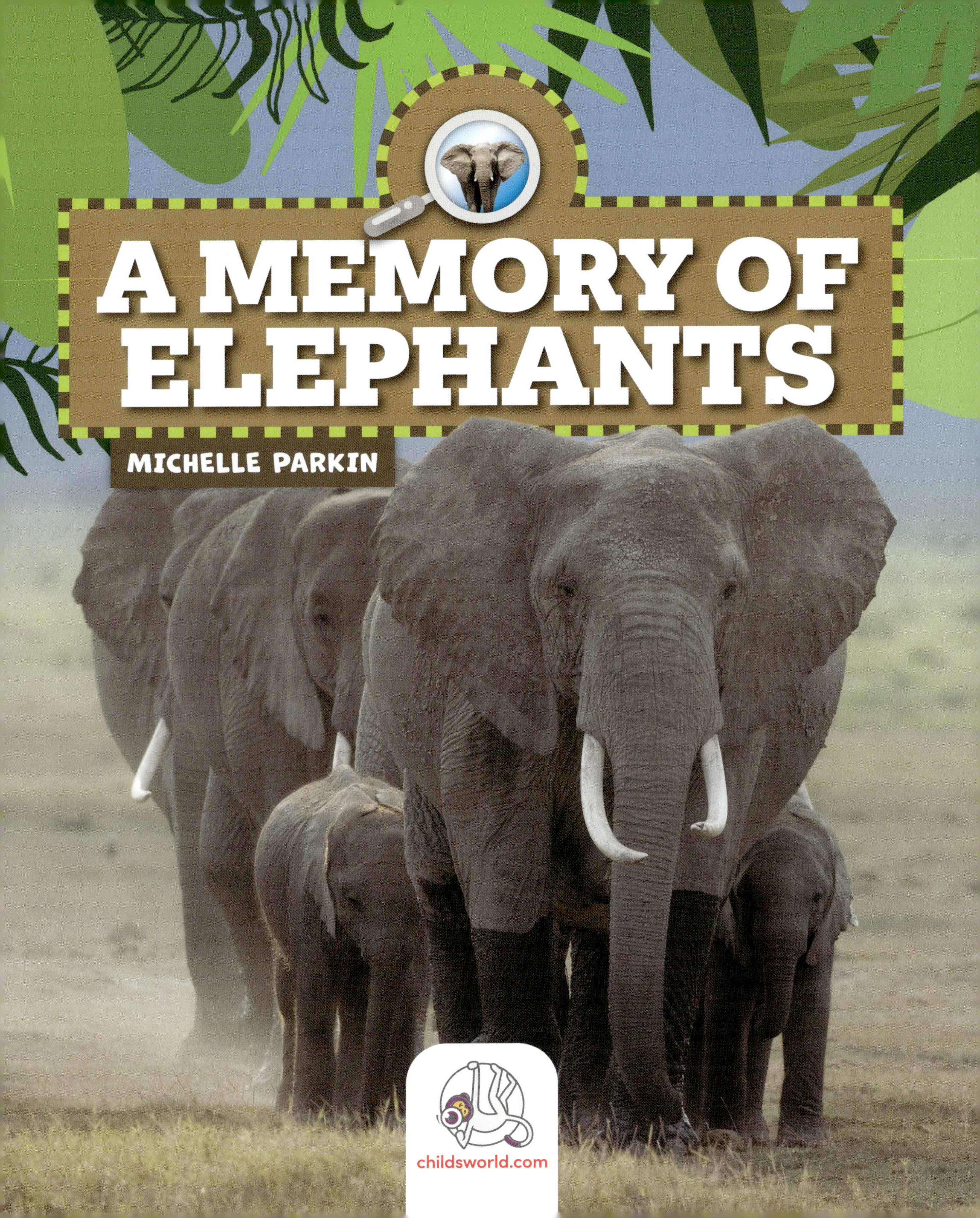
A MEMORY OF
ELEPHANTS
MICHELLE PARKIN
childsworld.com

Published by The Child's World®
800-599-READ • www.childsworld.com

Photography Credits
page 1: ©johan63/Shutterstock; page 1: ©Anastasiia Verych/Shutterstock; page 1: ©Jeff Grabert/Shutterstock; page 5: ©adogslifephoto/Getty Images; page 11: ©Wirestock/Getty Images; page 12: ©Anup Shah/Getty Images; page 14: ©Vicki Jauron, Babylon and Beyond Photography/Getty Images; page 17: ©Simoneemanphotography/Getty Images; page 18: ©THANH NGUYEN/Contributor/Getty Images; page 20: ©Diana Robinson/Getty Images; page 22: ©Dorling Kindersley: Ruth Jenkinson/Getty Images

ISBN Information
9781503884953 (Reinforced Library Binding)
9781503885851 (Portable Document Format)
9781503886490 (Online Multi-user eBook)
9781503887138 (Electronic Publication)

LCCN 2023937348

Printed in the United States of America

Michelle Parkin is an editor and author. She has written more than 20 children's books and articles about famous people, animals, and dinosaurs. She lives with her daughter and goldendoodle in Minnesota.

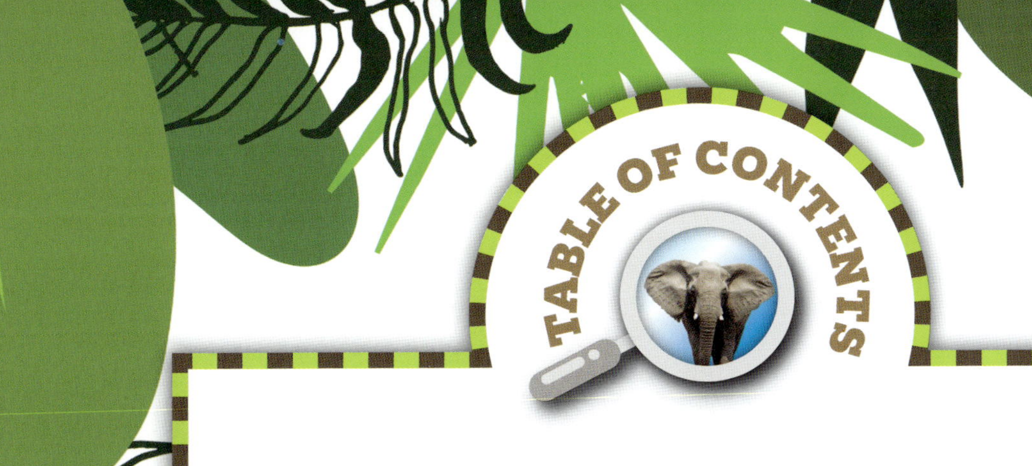
TABLE OF CONTENTS

Meet the Memory

It's a hot day on the African grassland. Suddenly, the ground starts to shake. Is it an earthquake? No, it's a group of African elephants walking toward a water hole in a long, straight line.

There are three kinds of elephants. They are African savanna elephants, African forest elephants, and Asian elephants. African savanna elephants are the largest. Both kinds of African elephants have much larger ears, shaped a little like the continent of Africa. Asian elephants' ears are smaller and rounder.

But all kinds of elephants have one thing in common—they live and travel in a group called a **herd**. A herd of elephants is called a memory.

ASIA
AFRICA
Atlantic Ocean
Indian Ocean
KEY
Where elephants live

A memory of elephants can walk up to 7.5 miles (12.07 kilometers) per day in search of food.

Elephants are social animals. They form family groups made up of between 6 and 20 elephants. The oldest female elephant is the leader of the family. She makes the decisions. She leads the memory from place to place in search of food and water. The rest of the memory walks behind her. Elephant memories sometimes combine to form larger herds of more than 100 elephants and their calves. If a memory gets too large, it might split into two groups. But the memories usually stay close to each other as they move from place to place. There is safety in numbers!

Female elephants spend their entire lives with their families. Most of the elephants in a memory are related. The leader is called the **matriarch**. Her grown daughters stay with her, even when they have babies of their own. These mothers, daughters, and sisters raise their young, look for food, and play together.

Male elephants stay with their memory until they are at least 10 years old. Then they leave their mothers and live on their own or form small groups with other male elephants. Small herds of male elephants are called **bachelor** groups. These might have up to 14 male elephants. Male elephants often travel close to the female group they were born into, but they do not mix with the females.

Elephant Size Comparison

African elephants weigh up to 9 tons (8.2 metric tons). They are 10 to 13 feet (3-4 meters) feet tall.

White rhinos weigh 2–3 tons (1.8–2.7 mt). They are up to 6 feet (1.8 m) tall.

CHAPTER 2

All in the Family

Male elephants are called bulls. Females are called cows. A baby elephant is called a calf.

When a male elephant is ready to **mate**, he travels away from his group to find a female elephant. This happens when males are around 20 years old. But once he mates with a female, he goes back to his small group or roams on his own. Male elephants do not help raise their calves.

A cow gives birth to one calf after 22 months. This is the longest pregnancy for a **mammal**. When an elephant is giving birth, the rest of the memory circles around her. They protect her and the calf from danger. After the calf is born, the older elephants use their feet and trunks to throw sand onto the baby's skin. The sand is like sunscreen and protects the newborn's skin from sunburn.

An elephant cow and her calf travel together.

Baby elephants are very playful and form close bonds by tumbling and playing together.

Although a memory of elephants is made up of mostly females, there are no single moms in the herd. Raising elephant calves is a group effort. The younger females are known as allomothers. These big sisters and aunts act as babysitters. They help the older elephants care for their young and help protect all of the calves in a memory. This helps them learn to be mothers to their own future calves.

Elephant calves are fully dependent on their mothers for up to three years. They play with the other young elephants in the memory. They **mimic** the older elephants, which helps them learn how to use their trunks and how to eat plants.

Who's in Charge?

The matriarch decides where the memory travels to find food. She warns the other elephants if there is danger. Since elephants can live to be up to 70 years old, the elephant leader has a lot of experience to share with her memory. She knows the best watering holes and the best feeding spots. She can hear danger coming sooner than the younger elephants because she has heard it many times before.

Elephants have no natural **predators** in the wild. But lions, hyenas, and crocodiles can attack calves and weak elephants. The leader alerts the group if there is danger nearby. Families protect each other. They growl and charge at predators. Elephants also use their strong trunks and sharp **tusks** to protect themselves.

The matriarch leads the memory and makes all of the important decisions.

ELEPHANT EATS

Elephant memories are nomadic. This means that elephants are always on the move. One reason for this is to look for food. Elephants are **herbivores**. They eat grass, roots, small plants, tree bark, leaves, and fruit. It takes a lot of food to fill up a memory of elephants. One adult eats up to 500 pounds (226.8 kg) of food each day. Elephants spend 14–18 hours per day eating. All that eating can wear down an elephant's teeth. Elephants have six sets of teeth. When one set wears down, another replaces it.

CHAPTER 4

What Makes a Memory Unique?

Elephant memories communicate with each other through roars, snorts, barks, grunts, cries, and low rumbles. They make trumpet sounds with their trunks when they are excited or to signal danger.

Memories form close bonds and friendships. They help each other solve problems. Elephant families show their love by wrapping their trunks around each other like a hug. An elephant that does not have a family group can have a shorter life span and suffer from depression. Elephants are one of the few animals besides humans that expresses grief and sadness. When a member of the memory dies, the other elephants gather around the body and touch it gently with their trunks.

Elephants form close friendships and enjoy spending time together.

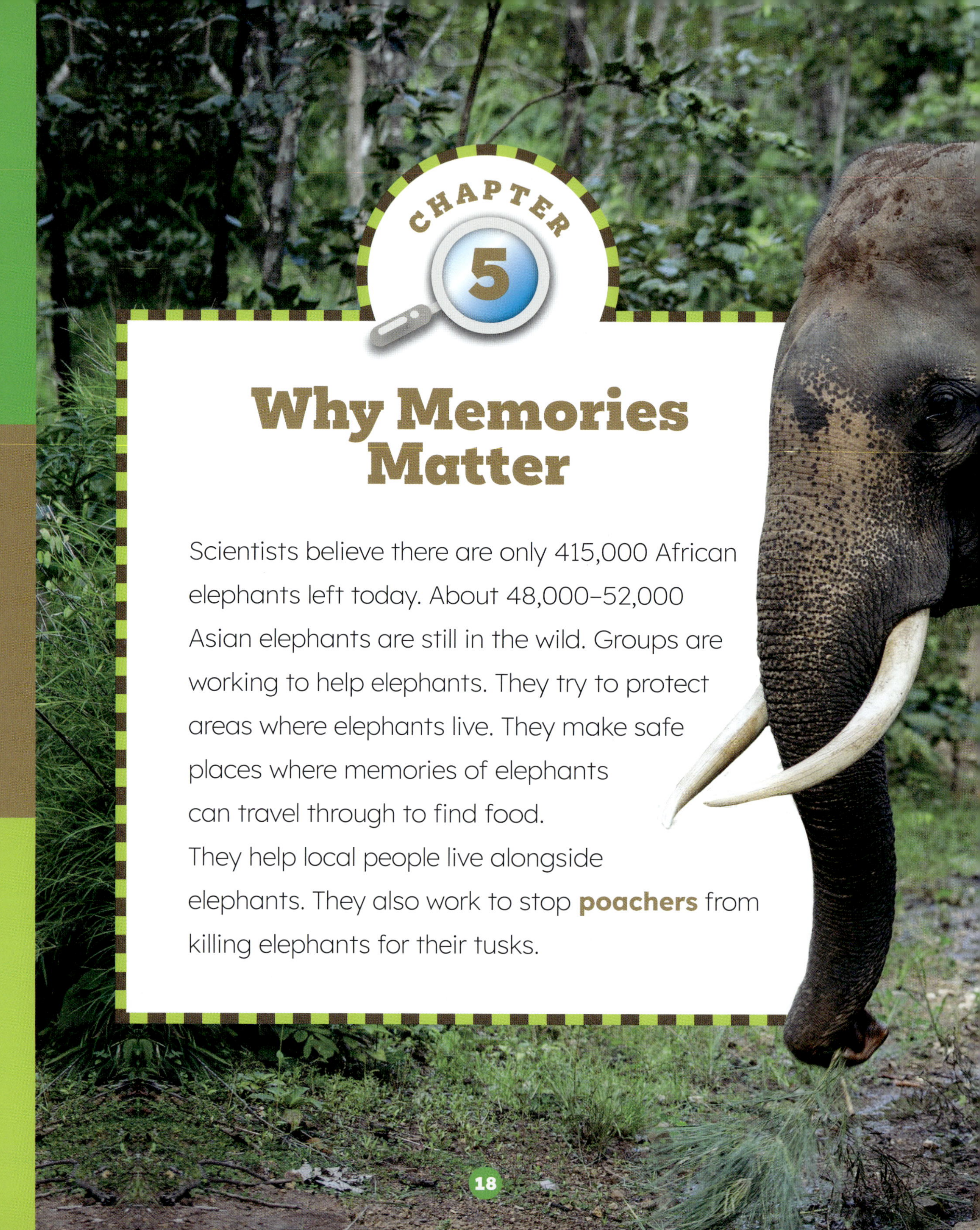

CHAPTER 5

Why Memories Matter

Scientists believe there are only 415,000 African elephants left today. About 48,000–52,000 Asian elephants are still in the wild. Groups are working to help elephants. They try to protect areas where elephants live. They make safe places where memories of elephants can travel through to find food. They help local people live alongside elephants. They also work to stop **poachers** from killing elephants for their tusks.

ELEPHANT MEMORY

People say an elephant never forgets. That might be true! Elephants have amazing memories. They can remember the faces of people and even other elephants they have met before. Scientists believe this is because of their large brains. The part of an elephant's brain responsible for processing memory is big compared to other animals. Having a good memory is especially important for . . . a memory of elephants! The matriarch remembers the best places to find food and water, and where dangerous predators might be. By showing the younger females these locations again and again, she helps them remember, too. In this way, an elephant's good memory helps keep the herd safe.

In protected areas such as this one, humans work closely with elephants and keep them safe.

Elephant memories are important to our world. The dung from large groups of elephants helps keep soil healthy. The fruits and plants that elephants eat contain seeds. The seeds are spread along the soil as memories travel. Memories make paths for other animals when they walk through thick forests. An elephant's large footprints fill with rainwater. These prints make homes for tadpoles and other tiny animals. And elephants are amazing examples of the importance of families working together. Hopefully, elephants will be around for years to come.

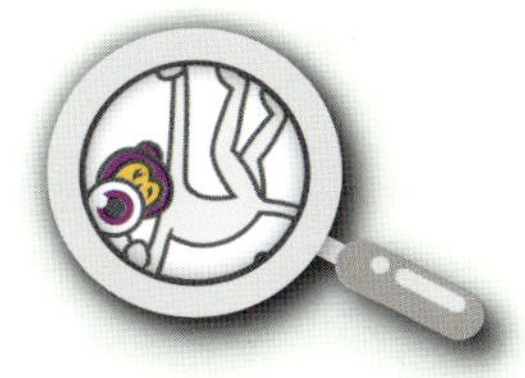

Wonder More

Wondering about New Information

What new information did you learn about elephant memories? Write down three new facts you learned. Did this information surprise you? Why or why not?

Wondering How It Matters

Why do you think it is important to learn about elephant memories? What can we learn about helping others from these unique families?

Wondering Why

Why do you think memories of elephants are important? What do you think would happen if the elephants died out? Think of one thing that could help elephants.

Ways to Keep Wondering

What questions do you have about elephant memories? Where could you go to find out more about them?

Make Your Own Elephant

Make your own elephant with this craft project you can do at home.

What You Need:

- One empty toilet paper roll
- Construction paper
- Paint (pick your favorite color)
- Paintbrush
- Black marker
- Scissors

Steps to Take:

1. Draw two elephant ears and a trunk on the construction paper. Cut them out.
2. Paint the trunk, ears, and toilet paper roll with your paintbrush. Let dry.
3. Once the paint has dried, glue the ears and trunk onto the toilet paper roll. Bend the trunk to give it a slight curve.
4. Take your black marker and draw eyes, lines on the trunk, and a tail in the back. Now you've made your own elephant!

Glossary

bachelor (BATCH-uh-lur) A bachelor is a male human or animal who does not have a partner.

herbivores (HUR-buh-vorz) Herbivores are animals that eat plants rather than other animals.

herd (HURD) A herd is a large group of the same type of animal that live and travel together.

mammal (MAM-uhl) A mammal is a warm-blooded animal with a backbone. A baby mammal drinks its mother's milk.

mate (MAYT) When animals mate, they join together to produce offspring.

matriarch (MAY-tree-ark) A matriarch is the female leader of a family, group, or organization.

mimic (MIH-mik) To mimic someone or something is to copy a behavior or trait.

poachers (POH-churz) Poachers are people who hunt and kill animals illegally.

predators (PRED-uh-turz) Predators are animals that live by hunting other animals for food.

tusks (TUSKS) Tusks are the pair of long, curved, pointed teeth on an elephant.

Find Out More

In the Library

Ihwagi, Dr. Festus W. *African Elephant: A First Field Guide to the Big-Eared Giant of the Savanna.* New York, NY: Neon Squid, 2022.

Jenkins, Steve, and Robin Page. *Why Do Elephants Have Big Ears? Questions—and Surprising Answers—About Animals.* New York, NY: Little, Brown Books for Young Readers, 2023.

Thomson, Sarah L. *Save the ... Elephants.* New York City, NY: Philomel Books, 2022.

On the Web

Visit our website for links about elephant memories:
childsworld.com/links

Note to Parents, Caregivers, Teachers, and Librarians: We routinely verify our web links to make sure they are safe and active sites. So encourage your readers to check them out!

Index